Writing for Fun and Pocket Change

By

Susan Devine Napoli

This book was written for information and does not promise or imply that you will be a successful writer or make any money at it.

Table of Contents

Introduction

Like most anyone else who loves the arts, I had dreams of big money. I even picked out a penthouse in town on the internet when I uploaded my first book on Amazon. That dream makes me laugh too.

I started writing because I had learned how to bind one signature books in a class at the university on Art for Elementary School Teachers. It seemed funny to do this and not have anything written in them. A few weeks later my friends on my floor in the dorm were buying Christmas presents for their families and I had little money to do that so I decided to write and hand bind my first book. It cost about $7.00 to make a copy for each person in my family and a lot of time. A girl on the floor typed it up for me for free from my handwritten copy. My family loved it. They wanted more. Time to time, I wrote another and then another. Soon I wanted to write a book to sell. That is when the real adventure began.

Come along and let me share some tips about how not to invest money in your book and enjoy getting it into print. There is a lot of trickery in this industry for people who really just want to hold something they are proud of in their hands and say "I did this." To have something to display and participate in a signing and talk about writing is a wondrous thing most anyone can enjoy. If you want to know how to write a best seller, this is not your book. No one can promise you that. This is all about writing for fun.

Part 1: Getting Started

Writing for fun can bring so much pleasure. It is really very simple. You probably wrote stories in school. You probably had to read things you either did or didn't like. All that counts. You would not have bought this book if you didn't get some success or pleasure from some aspect of it.

Like many smart people, some sources and authors make it sound too hard. I think it is excellence they are striving for. That in itself is not a bad thing. But to start by trying to achieve excellence is like getting up off the couch after not exercising and going to the Olympics and expecting to get a metal on the first attempt.

The media is no help with this. There are feature stories and shows that make it look like all it takes is a little bit of effort to achieve greatness. They usually leave the hard work part out. They allude to it but asking such questions like "How long have you been doing this?" Then the person being interviewed says, "I started when I was four." There is not much discussion about that usually. What it means is that was when the process began that they began to practice. From then until the moment they are be interviewed there was some intensive stuff going on that nobody cares to hear about. Their starts and stops and frustrations and tears. There were times when nobody believed in them. Then one day it became like breathing to them and they forgot about what it was like to be a beginner. This makes the interview go really well. Then the next question is about how they got their big break. That is the best story ever. The journalist is satisfied that they got their story.

As an educator, I know that learning happens in small increments for everyone. The rate people learn at varies greatly.

It has to do with how motivated they are to learn it, the skills they come with, and the opportunity to get support as they practice. It is very possible also for someone to get quite good at something that, in the beginning, looked terrible. I am not saying that anyone can master anything. Sometimes people can't for lots of reasons. Other times they are the underdog just waiting to be given the "Hail Mary Pass" after all the practice no one noticed. Whatever the case, you can get some enjoyment out of writing if you really want to.

This part of the book has the basics of what you need to do to get started. You are off on an adventure....

Where do ideas come from?

I do not know. Getting your idea that you can commit hours upon hours working on is a project all in itself. You have several options: you could piggy back off something you love that you have read, you could take several ideas and combine them to be your own, or you could come up with something new.

They say there are no new ideas, that every story has been written. It seems so perusing the bookstore. So the Twilight series came out and suddenly many people are writing vampire love stories. You can do that, it is always an option.

You could take several ideas and put them together. My favorite is the Roger Housdon poetry books. He did not write the poems, he compiled them into themes and wrote about each poem he found that he loves. His love for the poetry comes through in his explanations. He has excellent taste in poetry and parts of poems. It is fresh and lovely. You could do that too with something you love.

The last option is to come up with something new like the Harry Potter series. JK Rowling broke a lot of "rules" with that first book. I never read anything so dark that was for children. She exceeded the page limitations publishers thought children could read. The guidelines then were about 200 pages. She topped out at over 800 pages. Critics said the children would never read it. They did and loved it.

One thing to note about ideas is that they cannot be copyrighted. The copyright office is the first one to say that. If you talk about your ideas, then they are for anyone who hears them. I am very wary of online websites that have authors share as they write and people can read it before it is published and copyrighted. I suggest you keep your ideas to yourself. As a beginner I would get all excited about an idea and then tell somebody about. What happened was worse than someone stealing it. I gave away the magic of what I was doing, lost interest in it and never finished.

Another thing about ideas is that sometimes people are inspired and someone else has almost the same idea who is someplace else. They do not know each other or know about the other's idea. This is called zeitgeist. It is surprising how frequently this happens.

People have gone to court over who took whose ideas and profited or infringed on copyright. Even trying to use the brand name of a product in your story is a problem. Ideas are people's property. Don't take copyrighted material and call it yours if it is not. This is called plagiarism. The ability to copy and paste can make this extremely easy. People have lost jobs, gotten kicked out of college, and embarrassed in the media for plagiarism. Many people will give permission if an acknowledgement is requested and an agreement is made as to how much of theirs you want to use.

On the other hand, there are acceptable ways you can use other people's ideas and build on them such as in fan fiction. This is usually the follow up to a well-known work and people like to come up with new stories the established characters are placed in. One example is the Harry Potter series has a lot of fan fiction. Last time that I looked online there was a website with over 80,000 pieces of writing on there and 40,000 on another. Fan Fiction is now a new genre.

Another acceptable way is to make a parody or satire of an established piece. There is a zombie series that changes the classic literature like Jayne Eyre. Such classics are now public domain and anyone can use them in this way without copyright infringement because the copyright has run out.

All of this can get so tricky and sticky that there are attorneys that specialize in the arts. You can always seek advice from such an attorney if you have questions. Usually such information can be gained at writing conferences and workshops is enough to the beginning writer.

The best advice I have for all of this is to keep your eyes and ears open. Sometimes it takes just a little bit of something to cause an idea to grow.

Beginning to Write

People who do not write want to know about the apparent "magic" they see in front of them. They want to know the secrets so that they too can write something. Some people will copy what other writers do and hope to get the same success. It is not what they do but what they produce that makes them a writer. In my estimation, it works best when you allow you to be you.

One of the things that matters is if the person can tolerate working alone for periods of time. Some people can and some people can't. This is hugely discouraging to people who cannot tolerate the long quiet hours. Writing is slow tedious work and a labor of love.

Some simple equipment is all that is needed to get started writing. Most writers work on a computer these days. This is especially helpful to self-publishers because when you are finished you have an electronic copy that can be easily formatted and uploaded to your on demand publisher.

There are fewer rules today about manuscript lengths than in previous times. Some magazines have only so much space in their publication so it is important to follow those guidelines. Mostly though, book writing can be short or long. My particular on demand publisher requires a minimum of 50 pages. That includes all of the written pages including title pages, introduction, drawings, appendices...everything. If you tend to go long, it might be necessary to divide it up into a series or volumes.

The amount of time you spend and when is up to you too. Some creative folks work at night, some in the day. Some are all finished before noon. Others don't begin until late in the afternoon. Some can produce a book in a few months. Others work on it for years. All of this is highly individual and it is entirely up to you.

Write What You Know

I was in a high school painting class. My art teacher suggested we look at magazines to inspire us about what we wanted to paint. I brought in a photograph of a mountain. I started my painting and it went pretty well until I got stuck. She asked me about the light on the mountain snow. I couldn't answer. She asked me if I had ever been to the mountains. I said I hadn't. I learned that day to use what is familiar to me. So the next project I brought in a squash from our garden. She loved it. It took a good while to translate this in my writing.

Nicholas Sparks' stories take place in the eastern US coast, most all of them do because he lives there. He also has handwritten letters in them because he is old enough to have enjoyed writing and receiving letters himself. When I go to his movies I look for the setting and the letters. In one story, <u>Nights in Rodanthe</u>, he has hurricane preparation in it and the couple falls in love during the storm. I love that story. I have been through enough storms to know this is quite plausible.

Elizabeth Gilbert's books could take place most anywhere because she is a world traveler. It is a love for her and it was her solution to how to recover from divorce in her book <u>Eat, Pray, Love</u>. She did what she loved and then wrote about it. So many people loved the story that they got on airplanes with the hope that if they did what she did they might get the same results. Now that is a storyteller.

Read Voraciously

People who write have a love for the written word in all forms. They fell in love with a book at some point and they dove into new worlds. Both my kids fell in love with reading because I love reading. I read to them when they were very young. I knew I had succeeded when I took my son to the bookstore and he finished reading the book I bought him on the way home 20 minutes away. After that, we went to the library. When they really loved a book, I would buy them their own copy when I could. They didn't have any trouble learning to read. But I did.

I had a rough start with learning to read in first grade. I had to practice at home in the kitchen while my mom cooked dinner. Then again in 7th grade my mom noticed me having trouble and brought home a biography on Harriet Tubman and sat next to my bed every night. I didn't want to but she would not take no for an answer. She read a page and then I did until I caught up. After that, it went pretty well.

She made us read all summer, every summer. We went to the library every week. I have five younger brothers and sisters. The library let us take as many as ten books each. Our family alone was responsible for some great circulation numbers thanks to my mom.

All this reading has helped me to love the written word and increase my vocabulary. I learned that one should write what they love to read.

All this reading does influence the kind of writing people do. As people read, they can see who the favorite authors are of the writer. I wrote a children's story and the feedback was that it was Toy Story meets the Velveteen Rabbit. I loved that. I didn't know such a thing could happen. I was afraid of plagiarizing by accident for a good while and then learned about influences and never thought about plagiarism again.

Today I have what I call a "book day" from time to time. I go looking at resale shops for books, nothing like getting a book for a dollar. Then I move on to the discounted book places. After that I move on to the bookstore. I also go to the library. It is in the library I find I am the most adventurous. I can go into new sections and check out books I would not ordinarily buy. Sometimes I do all of this and come home empty handed. Sometimes I come home with an armload full. The joy for me is in the hunt.

There are online books to hunt for too. That involves having to wait for the books to come in. There are lots of books that are not as popular as you find in the bookstore and just as good. Last summer I found free e-books. Now I can download a book to my phone for free and in seconds it is mine. Yeah, I like that very much. Once I was waiting for hours at a hospital for someone to get back the results of a test. She was on her phone so I went on mine. After surfing the internet a little bit I got the idea to download a book. It was fantastic to be able to do this.

Go to Writing Workshops and Classes

Find out what other authors do to craft a story. I have been to several. It is a lot of fun to find out about the process and meet new people and thumb through their work. People who attend these are usually quite open about what they do and are willing to help. I learned from attending a puppet workshop weekend with my mom when I was nineteen that it is okay to tell people that you are just beginning and came to learn.

Choose workshops and classes that come from reputable places. I went to one at Rice University as part of their continuing education program for 5 days one summer. I went to several sponsored by a writer's guild. These had manuscript reviews that tell the truth about your writing and how you might make it better. They seek to educate and to encourage for a nominal fee. I came away with ideas of all kinds. I got better over time.

When I was in college I was sent to the writing center there where I learned what my mistakes in grammar and mechanics were. I absolutely hated that experience but I learned the mistakes I made regularly. This too is extremely valuable.

◊◊◊

Part 2: Sharing Your Writing

Now that you have finished a piece of writing you might want to share it. There are lots of ways to share writing that both you and the reader can enjoy. A lot of famous people have done that even at the beginning. I learned that the singer John Denver made an album of his own songs that he designed and produced for just family and friends for a gift long before he became popular and had a record label. Think about ways you might want to start sharing your writing.

It is quite simple to get help with making copies at copy shop. They know how to print what you wrote. There are lots of ways they can bind it and present it. The trick with this is it can get expensive easily. The more you have them do the more expensive it gets. What I did at the beginning was bring in the pages laid out in the order and fashion I wanted them to appear in the finished book. I wanted them to be printed on both sides of the page. This meant a lot of figuring and taping the smaller pages on to a large one. When I took it to the copy shop I only paid for them to hand set the pages I gave them. They ran a sample and then had me check it. I learned that page numbers make for very quick checking. In minutes I had the interior of my little book for several copies. I took the interior pages home and hand bound my little books. I particularly like the artistry part of this. I like to make my little books beautiful. This is particularly nice for gift giving. Over time I have inserted beads and charms in the binding. It is pretty and makes it unique.

This may be all that you want to do for a time. These little books make great inexpensive gifts that friends and family might like. It is fun to sign them and personalize them.

Be sure to put a copyright notice in it before you print. This lets people know that you are serious about your writing and it protects it. Even family and friends don't get how much work you put into it sometimes. You might want to put a little notice about asking you for permission to use your writing. It is so easy today for them to take it to a copy machine to share with others without your permission. Remember, you cannot control what people do once you put it out there. It can take on a life of its own that you didn't expect. Even at these early stages.

Part 3: Going Public

Going public is a huge step for lots of writers. It means a number of things.

1) That you have written for a particular audience
2) That you believe in yourself
3) That you think it will sell

This takes a lot of homework to investigate the market and your audience. My first venture was pretty successful for what is called a "Niche" piece. I sold 379 copies.

Here Come the Wolves in Sheep's Clothing

Just saying you have a book written or talk about an idea for one brings out the wolves. These people do not create or cannot come up with their own ideas, so they steal it, some with a smile. This happened to me at a workshop. I talked with someone showing her this idea I had I was going to create puppets that went with children's stories. The next time I saw her she had the book she wrote with all the puppets. I couldn't believe it. She had taken my idea! I learned to keep my ideas to myself.

Some will try to trick you as they are savvy business people looking for the people who don't know. They design programs and websites and make promises they cannot keep. These people will take all of your profits and not turn back. I have two such examples.

I had heard a story of the author of The Little Engine that Could sold her story for $400 and gave away all rights to it when I attended a writing conference. When I did some fact checking, I found out that this was not true but a cautionary tale to help us keep our rights to our work.

Sarah Ban Breathnach wrote Simple Abundance and it was a huge bestseller. She went on the Oprah Winfrey Show several times. She was savvy and innovative in so many ways. Then she married a man who soaked her for every penny. Read her account of how this happened in Peace and Plenty. This is important reading for those of you on the Rich and Famous Track.

Looking for a Publisher

Seeking a publisher takes a lot of time and effort. You can read about how many famous books got rejected and what they said about particular books and authors. Finding a "real" publisher is a struggle. I should know, I never could get one. I had a chance once and never recognized it. I sent a children's story to a publisher. I got a letter back asking for a few changes. It hurt my feelings and I never replied. Years later, at a workshop I learned that if you get such a letter, they like it. I was crushed. Every submission of some of the 73 pieces I wrote after that was rejected. Every. One. The publisher's name was Harper & Row, now known as Harper Collins. Sigh.

I learned a lot from all those rejection letters like to never send out a rough draft of anything. I learned to look at the kind of books each company publishes and not to bother them with something they just don't do. There are publications and lists that can steer you. These lists get out of date quite quickly and companies get merged or go under. It is long tedious work. Most companies like a well thought out query letter so that they can request to see the manuscript if they are interested. Many companies don't want to hear from you unless you have an agent, so don't.

There are also companies that look like publishers but are not. These are called vanity presses. I learned at a workshop that a real publisher will pay you for your work. Vanity presses will charge you for their services and make you take the risk. They are actually book manufacturers. They make their money from printing books and all the services they offer to make it look good. They edit it. They put it through the normal cycle of getting a book to market. They don't care if it is a good book or not. They go with the author's desire to see themselves in print. These companies then have a minimum print order. That is where it gets tricky. The more "vain" the author is about the quality of the book, the more copies they can talk you into printing, hence the title vanity press. The reality is often much different than the perception that the author gets from these "publishers".

Before you get completely discouraged with this idea, I have two examples for you. The story the "Night before Christmas" was indeed a self-published book. I know you know that story. The second one is This Time I Dance by Tama Kieves. She was a lawyer and was miserable so she quit her job to pursue her passion of writing. She wrote and self-published her book while waiting tables. She got the call one day that this editor found her book and loved it and wanted to publish it. She was elated. It became a best seller.

Personally, I never had the money to afford such a hefty bill for printing a book. I am a teacher by trade and that kind of money just isn't available. At the time, I could not picture myself marketing and selling my own book. My Dad had an agreement with such a company in secret. When he died my mom found it and now she has to deal with the company and get the book out. Since the books were paid in full, she has to decide what to do. Will she print or not? Hummm...

My first Self-Publishing Venture

Self-publishing is another option for those that want to see their work in print. It can be very expensive or not depending on how much you want to do. I decided to go this route because I knew my audience and how to reach them. My first self-published book was <u>A Fiesta of Ideas: a curriculum on Mexico</u>. It was a book for teachers of young children. What had happened was there was a trend on multiculturalism and no material on the market for teaching children about culture so I wrote one. I had been to workshops and conventions and was a preschool teacher myself. I had noticed others giving it a try too.

I wrote and illustrated the book, developed the teaching materials, and put together a display. I gave workshops on it at all the conventions. I went to an autograph party at a convention too. I got paid about $35 for each of the workshops. I got approached by a school supply catalog and they wanted to put it in their multicultural kit. I agreed and came up with a wholesale price. They ordered about one hundred at a time. I made several hundred dollars.

 The convention folks got wise to all of us doing this and made it a rule that we could not promote our books at a training. They didn't want it to be a commercial for out books but for the participants to learn something. Mine was pretty good so I just didn't mention I had a book unless a participant asked. The final blow came when I went back to work and my boss' boss came in and congratulated me about my book and had me sign something that said I could not write about work things from this workplace. The book I wrote was from a previous workplace. It crushed me. This was a brush with intellectual property that I was not aware of.

I wrote another book called <u>Puppets for One and All</u>. I took it to the local puppet guild convention. It was received okay but not many of the participants were teachers. Most of the audience was puppeteers or librarians. A woman approached me about putting my book in her shop. I sent her 12 copies. I never got a check or got them back. She closed her store.

I started a book on working with two year olds in the new workplace that I signed the agreement on but I never finished it. I got super discouraged realizing I could not write about work and stopped for a long time. I didn't really understand intellectual property. All I could see was that I was a child care provider with a degree trying to make a living on a low salary. I never wrote another book that was work related again for many, many years.

I did give a workshop on working with two year olds at the national convention. It was standing room only. The hall got so packed that the Fire Marshall came in and took people out. The room held about 400. After the presentation, a publisher approached me about writing a book. Her company had a format to follow that I didn't like. I never wrote the book. I went back to writing for my family.

As I think back on those first self-publishing experiences, it had some difficulties that I remember. The copy shop tried to tell me if they printed it, it was theirs. I told them I held the copyright on it. They stopped with that and still took my printing orders. I never knew when an order was coming in and the timing was not always good with my life. I had a newborn baby at the time and found it difficult to drop everything and fill the orders. In order to make money on them I had to bind them myself. I got a little plastic binding machine and did it myself.

This led to a few messed up books that I couldn't sell. The checks didn't always go through on the individual orders. I learned to let the check clear before I sent out a book after losing a few. I learned if I sent a book out for review, they never returned it. People wanted it for free and were open about it. One lady went as far as tracing something from it on a display. I should have charged her a dollar. There was a general lack of respect by those that didn't get the time and energy it took to create it.

I also had a really good time with those that loved my book. I got treated like a celebrity twice. "I know you, you wrote that book. It really came at a time when I really needed it." said one. The other was so awestruck to be in my presence that it made me uncomfortable. We chatted and she walked away on clouds.

Displays and Autograph Parties

When putting together a display it can be very simple: a new table cloth to cover the table where you will sit that complements the color of your book, a sign introducing who you are, contact information, a means for taking money both cash and card, and a pen for signing books with.

The display should not detract from your book. My first one was all handmade. I had items imported from Mexico on it. I wore a colorful hand embroidered dress that was popular at the time. I never really sold much at that time in the way of orders but I did get in a school supply catalog. I learned too that some places charged for putting a table out and it was way more than I had the confidence of selling for that particular time period. I had cards made up. Most people if they want the book, want it now and make it clear. Many of those will not order it later. That is just how it goes. I was never one for printing large quantities of my books to sell. I had heard of stories of people with large quantities of books dry rotting in the garage. I didn't want to be one of those authors.

After the display is together it is best to think about a few things: can you tell what you book is about in two sentences? Can you tell the story of the story and how it came to be? Can you talk about your love of writing and your creative process? What approach are you going to take? Hard sell? Soft sell? It is best to plan out what to say ahead of time.

In regards to autographing, now called signing, the actual book, what will you write? It is good to plan that out too. I have seen everything from the author's initials in red to authors with a slogan or even drawing a picture. My skeptical Dad told me once to never sign with the signature you use to sign checks. He thought people would use it to forge his signature on things. As I look around at signatures on things like sports memorabilia and books his advice appears to be true. Whatever you choose it should be quick to produce and people will most likely talk to you while you sign. You have to be able to do both at the same time. Consider ahead of time whether you will sign books with people's names in them or not. If you misspell it you are sunk. Do not personalize a book that is not paid for. If you do and they don't pay, nobody wants it.

Taking money should be a smooth transaction and give you a record of the sales. A big thing right now is the swipe mechanism that can be added to one's smart phone. It goes straight to your bank and the transaction is approved before you let them have the book. They get an e-receipt too. I would have loved this in the 1980's. Fewer people carry cash. Practically no one takes a check. Signal failure is a problem with this occasionally. I have one and I haven't used it yet.

◊◊◊

Part 4: Going Really Big with Print on Demand

The Oprah Effect

As a fan of the Oprah Winfrey show for about 20 years I learned quite a lot about myself. It was during a show on Lifestyle Makeover that I decided I wanted a new life and started working on it. Lots of things happened. I walked away from my marriage and moved into an apartment to try and figure things out. I heard a show of Joan Anderson speaking about her experience with walking away from her life in her book <u>A Year by the Sea</u>. It appeared I had company with such feelings. I got serious about a lot of things. By this time Oprah's Book Club was in full swing.

Over time I went from watching the readers swoon over books to wanting to become one of her authors. A few minutes on the show and they sold millions of copies. She loved books and authors. She had single handedly turned the publishing world upside down by just saying she liked someone's book. Authors were sending her their book. I wanted her to like a book of mine too. Her endorsement of a book or product made people successful overnight. Sales went as high as 1000% better when she said, "I want one of these." This has become known as the Oprah Effect.

Enter the Internet

During my seemingly writing hiatus I never really stopped writing. I did a lot of journaling. Lots. I would figure stuff out in there. Then a thought came to me to write something I can sell from seemingly nowhere. It caught me by surprise. Then some encouragement.

I had been trying to write something. I had actually started several times but it wasn't right. I also had a fiction piece that took on a life of its own and I got stuck. Two weeks before the end of my summer vacation, I decided to try the one I kept trying to write. I had gotten stuck in wanting it to be chronological and abandoned that. I decided to just tell the story. I sat down to my computer and the words came flying out of my fingers. Nothing had ever happened to me like that before. In two weeks the rough draft was done. I was exhausted and happy. It was fifty pages. I knew that it was not long enough, or so I thought.

I found an article that said a particular author suggested writers take a year to edit the rough draft. So I did. I checked it and let it sit over and over again for the entire year. I then went looking for a publisher. I bought the Writer's Market and went at it. I discovered that publishing had changed a lot. I was aware of the mergers of the companies. I searched and found all the big companies had no more slush pile (unsolicited manuscripts the lowest editors read in hope of finding something good that came in the mail). So I wrote query letters and e-mailed them. Just like before, they don't like multiple submissions. They can take as long as months of waiting to hear from them. I spent two years doing this. It was five or six rejections. I got form letter type e-mails and then came the last one. It said that they reject far too many good books and that they are a small press and publish a limited number of titles and wished me luck. It was definitely a rejection but it gave me hope. There was something good about this book. They didn't say what. That was enough for me. I decided to self-publish <u>Taking Care of Susan</u>. Off to the copy shop I went. It was so exciting and terrifying. I printed ten copies and decided my book would be art too so I went home and hand bound it adding beads in the binding. I designed a folio to put each copy in and numbered them. Each cover I made by hand. I put it up on Etsy with my puppet book I still had copies of. I didn't sell any. I went to a religious retreat and talked about my book briefly one night as we chatted over popcorn on the patio. They loved that I wrote a book. One of them bought a copy that I sent to her later. I was so excited that I sent it fast instead of book rate. I made no money on the sale of that book. Sigh. It was happening again.

There was a fear that never subsided. It just nagged at me all this time. I sat down and edited it one last time and felt much better about it. I didn't want to include my ex in it as much and some other things that left me feeling like I said too much. It was much better. Another surprising thought came.

Think bigger.

As I looked around for a bigger place for my book to go, it got pretty exciting.

Think bigger.

Encouragement came as I went from one idea to another.

Bigger.

I looked and looked. I went to a training at work at another campus and there was a poster on the wall of a woman who took a continuing education course there and had some success at selling a book of recipes she developed. They were recipes of desserts she made one serving at a time in a coffee cup she microwaved when her husband was not home. It was a delightfully good idea. I wrote down her name and went online to see what I could find out about her. She lived very close by. I wrote her an e-mail and asked her if we could meet for lunch and talk about books. She said yes.

So for the price of my own sandwich I got a great conversation and introduced to Create Space, an Amazon company. There it was...big, really big. I went home and bought her ebook for five dollars on self-publishing. She invited me to her writer's group which I could not attend because of my work schedule. I thanked her. The workplace that made me sign and stop writing had unwittingly given it back.

I looked over the Create Space website. She had said that she self-published for free. She said that there were other options but that she always did the free version. I saw what she meant. I also saw that the minimum was 50 pages. I felt like I had found my place. There were lots of directions to click on. The dashboard across the top checked off everything as I went. I made my own cover with the cover creator. I uploaded the manuscript and hit send for the review of what I had submitted. I made several mistakes and we went back and forth with them until I got it right.

I then had to open an account for my royalties to go in to. Amazon preferred electronic deposit. They do everything for me. When someone orders a book they print it and send it. No more trips to the post office. No more packaging materials to buy. No more losses from bouncy checks. I got to set my own price. They were very clear on their cost and I could charge what I wanted after that. There was no negotiation. They accepted my price with no problem. I later was offered to sell in Europe so I clicked yes. I got a few sales in the British pounds and the Euros. Amazon not only shipped there, they took care of the money exchanging. Only US dollars went in my account. It was so exiting to load a book while I was on vacation and watch the sales reports come in as I worked my day job. The only cost I incurred was the price of the proof which was about $3.00 plus shipping.

The proof coming in the mail was so exciting it was almost surreal to me. I couldn't believe I was holding my book. Finally, after all this time, I was in print. Yes, me and my new best friend Amazon, finally did it.

All the while, I had hoped to be one of Oprah's authors and there was talk about her closing the show. My book had finally become available 4 months before the show ended. It was too late. Me and Amazon would have to do it ourselves.

I loaded 4 more books. I found out about kindle Direct Publishing, another Amazon company. The book purist in me wanted pages to turn. Would I cross over and offer ebooks too? I wrestled with it and then I did, much to my own dismay. The options on there were even more so. Without a hard copy to mail, my readers could have it quick. I didn't sell many because the formatting was difficult to do and the margins were messed up. A few sold anyway. I discovered that ebooks can go to all the English speakers in the world. It was so amazing to look through all the reports from all the countries. Admittedly, most of them were zero sales most of the time but I got the process down on how to do it all.

Marketing

Then life happened and I met someone who also writes books. I saw that he is very good at marketing his work. I looked and looked at his stuff online. I loved his guts to even put his stuff out there. I loved his way in which he "pushes the envelope" creatively. At the time, I was super fearful of doing either of these things. I watched and studied. I thought about how I might market my work that would be unique to me.

I had a website that I paid $40 a year for. I had a lot of fun setting it up. I ended up using it to post my books and write about writing, mostly about being afraid to. Nobody was reading it. I sent a link to a magazine that I loved. I got some views, from the magazine staff I am sure, because month later the publisher wrote a piece on art and fear and how she didn't understand this, as art was like breathing to her. Then the views stopped and I didn't pay. It disappeared.

I decided that there must be free options because my new friend was using them. He was very, very careful of what he put out there creating an online image. I never thought of that. I think it is the first step in branding. I did not want to copy him. I wanted something of my own. I decided to write a blog that went with the books I wrote. I chose the one that is well known and free: blogger.

Setting it up was very easy. Early on I decided the blog should have a purpose. The first one was to record my writing journey. I got a few who were interested in that one. The second one went with my book. I decided I would write about what I do to take care of Susan, the title of my book. I put lots of things on there: places I visited around town, my love of tea, the antics of my cats, how I dealt with good and bad things happening, and how I relieved stress. My stats started lighting up. People logged on from all over the world. I got 97 views in 6 hours a few times. I posted every day. It was thrilling. Then one day, viewership dropped suddenly and never came back. I did realize that I was repeating and there wasn't really anything new to report. They saw that. I opened a new blog for each book as I got them done.

I ordered some blue plastic bracelets to go with one of my books that said "go slow, get there faster". I didn't do much with them. I wrote a book by the same name. It didn't sell.

I went to a 1 day workshop on marketing my book. They had us consider lots of things. One of them was that was I easy to find online? As she explained I realized I had a unique situation I spoke to her about on the break. My website was my name which was the same name as a 1986 centerfold. It became my name in 1987, when I got married. Whenever people google the name they get her, of course they do. I know you are laughing again. Me too. I just didn't know. So she helped me come up with a new website domain name "bookartcreations". There. It was the one I paid $40 a year for that I let expire.

I scraped up my guts and posted to my personal facebook to my friends and family about my books. A few liked it but not much. Then I made a facebook for just my writing. It is slow progress to write so I don't get many views or likes because I don't post much.

I made a workshop to go with my book which I am still developing. I intend that when I give it one day, I will slip a copy of my book in a tote bag for them to take home.

I went to an area store that sells handmade items of all kinds. I approached the owners about placing my book in their store. They said they would love to read it and consider it. I got no response and lost yet another book.

I approached a used bookstore about having a signing there. He said yes and said I would have to do the marketing. We picked a date and got it settled. He had told me he was not feeling well with a heart condition when I met him. He ended up closing the shop before my day. He apologized in an e-mail.

I approached another bookstore who had a summer of local author book signings. We sent emails back and forth. I gave her the link to my book preview on Amazon. I never heard back. I was smarter this time to not give away a hard copy of my book.

I met another author and daughter who helps her market her book. They got 1600 twitter followers in 2 weeks. That is major impressive. I thought of the area food trucks who use twitter like I saw in a movie. I am still considering that. I learned through them that there is an area coffee shop that supports the arts. The night I went there were authors signing and live music on the patio of a local band.

So all of these miserable stories are for a purpose; that success is hard won. I am okay with that. There is something about the struggle that makes success worthwhile. I know this from other things I have done and have succeeded at. It is very possible I haven't even written the good one yet, if there is such a thing. So for now, I am writing and learning as I go. In spite of it all, I am having the time of my life. The risk is low and I am learning to accept no as an answer better so there are no real mistakes here just a lot of learning going on.

When I get Discouraged or Blocked

Thankfully and sadly, writing is not my day job so when I get discouraged I put it down and walk away. I go to work. I walk. I paint. I make something. I visit family. I go to lunch with people. I talk with my artist friends over Pho (Vietnamese Noodle Soup). I clear my mind and then eventually come back to it. I have walked away many times and always, like a true love, it taps m on the shoulder and I come back to work on it a little more. I have been writing a long time.

As for unblocking, I can only speak for myself on this. I have a long mental list of the people who told me I cannot write. There were so many, mostly teachers I hate to admit, that said some really discouraging and unkind things. I have another group of people who do not support my efforts and at times have undermined me under the guise of fitting in and trying to contain my over the top creative spirit in lieu of being sensible and normal. I was terribly unhappy and either don't have them in my life anymore or I don't share what I am doing with them anymore. It is a wonder I write at all. Once I pulled away from all that mess, ideas started coming back. I listen to music with positive lyrics. My facebook feed is mostly all inspiration. For me, being blocked is a safety mechanism. When things are not emotionally safe in my life, my creativity goes underground and waits until the crisis has passed. As I think about this I realized many actors take time off when their lives turn upside down. After they make sense of it, they are back with a new book, album or movie.

I do have a philosophy about it all, that books have their own time to come into the world. The idea comes when it does, the process takes as long as it takes, and it is released into the world when it is time. I write whatever I want to write about. I allow myself to jump genres and styles if I want to. I don't care to develop it all into a platform at this point, it seems too limiting for the art I want to explore. I prefer nonfiction. It is natural for me because I am a teacher. I write because I have something to say.

Perfectionism

I tend to not be a perfectionist when it comes to writing. I know that drafts of a particular piece can be many. At first I kept track of the number of drafts and printed them. Not anymore. I tend to edit what I wrote the day before in case there are glaring errors that I won't understand what I meant to say when I read it later. Then when the entire first draft is done, I settle in to the tedious part that takes weeks and months.

I teach adults in my day job. A lot of their work is written. I read a lot of writing. Some folks are very perfectionistic about their writing. They really do expect to get it right on the first draft sometimes without even proof reading it. They are extremely hard on themselves if they don't get it perfect the first time. I allow for revisions of their work and some take me up on it. I give them the highest grade if they make thinks clearer or put in missing parts. Once I asked a young woman to revise and she got so angry she stormed out of the room and never came back. They don't know that people who write a lot and for a living know that this is simply part of the process.

Some people are very detail oriented and every single everything needs to be in place. True, some mistakes change the meaning. I just don't go there. I do the best I can and then move on to the next project.

Style

Each writer has their own style of writing about how they putt words together that is unique to them. I love this about writing. Over time and practice this develops and readers will recognize it is you that has written it.

One particularly famous author's style is Dr. Seuss. He has a rollicking and frolicking rhyming style that some writer's like so much they copy it. It is great to admire someone like that and many authors take it as a complement when that happens with their own. It is important to realize that doing that takes time and practice away from developing you own. Your approach to writing is really important for learning to reach <u>your</u> readers.

After Dr. Seuss' passing his wife granted permission to allow movies to be made of his work. I have seen a few. No one has even come close to his style. They found some of his unpublished work and are now publishing it. I have not been happy with any of it. He didn't publish it for a reason and is not here to say no. Don't they know that it needs to stay in the box?

Different types of writing require different styles. Technical writing for work is quite different from creative writing. Whatever the case, there is a place for you with your voice and your imaginings however creative or technical they are.

Flow and Other Seemingly Mystical Things About Writing

Writing is such an individual thing. There is no one right way to do it. Readers love the stories of how you write. Do you write long hand? On a computer? On an old typewriter? Do you write in a coffee shop? Do you have a designated place at home? Rent a hotel room? Do you eat or drink anything while you write? Do you travel to write? How deeply do you get into it? Do you experience flow as you write? Do you have a good luck charm of some sort? How much time in a day do you spend writing? How long does it take you to write a book? They love this stuff and will copy what you do hoping that it will help them succeed. It doesn't but it makes good marketing material.

I went to a lecture at the local university. It was the author of Forrest Gump, Winston Groom. Some people asked him questions alluding to these things. He wouldn't hear of it. He replied tersely, "Ass on the chair. Fingers on the keyboard." They didn't like his answer. They wanted a formula they could copy. He wouldn't give them one. It was quite a good talk in spite of this statement. He talked about things in the story and how it became a movie.

I also went to a lecture at my local community college and heard Richard Bach when I was in high school. He told how his bestselling story Jonathan Livingston Seagull came in a dream. He got up and wrote it all down but it was not complete. Later, he had another dream that finished the story. Amazing. I read a lot of his work. It probably did happen that way. He has a deeply spiritual side to him and his work. My favorite is Illusions: adventures of a reluctant messiah. I loved the book. In it was a mysterious little book that the character referred to by just opening it to a random page and it fit his situation perfectly. It must have created a lot of curiosity because in 2013, decades after the book came out, the little book did. I found it on Amazon and ordered it. When it came in and I opened the package there it was, small enough to fit in my hand and velveteen cover that remarkably looked like and felt like the one in the story to me. After all those years the magic of his story came back to me. I loved it. Interestingly, after looking it over quite well I realized that it was just a book of quotes from this story and his other stories. Just the same, it is a super intriguing idea that readers love.

As for flow, some authors get so involved with their work that they lose track of time and forget to stop and eat. It is not necessary part of writing but adds to the mystique of how it happens for some people.

There is quite a lot of talk about drug and alcohol use as part of getting ideas. It doesn't. There is even more talk about mental illness as part of the make-up of writers and artists. In reality, mental illness is quite common in society. We usually hear about those that get violent. The truth is, many people in all walks get up every morning and take their medicine and get on with life. They are not kept in insane asylums anymore or given horrible treatments. Sometimes artists of all kinds will use their art as a way of working through these really tough chapters in life and actually heal.

Many people don't understand the difference between divergent thinking and crazy. Divergent thinking is simply a process to which there are many answers to a question. This is hard on the convergent thinkers that think there must be one answer to questions. Through divergency, unique solutions can happen that surprise people. New trends come from this.

Movies and books come from this. Some are so far ahead of their time that it takes society a long time to appreciate and then love the new ideas. Some people think these new ideas are crazy. Truth is, the individual who is truly crazy doesn't really know they are and those with severe mental illnesses don't create during their horrible episodes. What you see that is different is really divergency. It is okay to be a writer.

The statement I like best regarding mental health and the highly creative individual comes from E. Paul Torrance a researcher. He said that when someone stops these individuals from creating is when the mental health problems occur, not the other way around as commonly perceived.

Knowing you own creative process is really important part of selling books. I studied creativity as part of a degree. We learned the research, explored our own creativity, and made a board game. We heard speakers. My favorite speaker was Story Musgrave, an astronaut who helped to fix the Hubble telescope after it was up in space. It was out of focus.The inspiration came from the shower fixture in the hotel in Europe where they were meeting. It had a sliding adjusting part of it that gave someone on the team the idea. They were able to adjust the telescope.

Luck is another mystical part of writing that many believe it. They come to depend on something that really has very little to do with the actual writing process. It is not a game of chance. People buy books because it interests them. What looks like luck is really mostly a game of skill. There is a lot of skill and determination in writing and book and then marketing it. Irregardless of who publishes the book, developing a following is needed. Traditional publishers call it developing a platform. They want to know about your expertise to write what you have written and that you are willing to do to promote it. This requires a lot of work and time. A self-publisher has to do the same. Sometimes incredible things happen in the process that look like luck but it has more to do with opportunity and to being ready for it. There are surprises in this which do look like luck both to the audience and the author. People really love to hear about these opportunities.

Comfort Zone

Each person has a comfort zone about what they are willing to do. One of the things I do when I write is continually step out of my comfort zone. That was not easy at first. I had a tight little life that was very predictable and I controlled everything I could to keep it that way. Then someone came along and reached beyond my defenses and I have not been the same since.

Little by little I tried new things going from small things like getting new clothes in a different style to trading my SUV for a Chevy Camaro. Then I changed a lot of what I did and started going on outings around my city. I tried new things as often as I could. Then I started getting better results creatively. Why? Because I put more and more of me into it.

I think back to a workshop on writing I attended and remember that was one of the points they stressed that week; you have to dig deep to the good stuff in order to write well. For me, that means stepping out of my comfort zone some. It has come to feel good to do this and something cool has happened. My comfort zone is getting bigger.

The Creative Space

Although it is not required, a creative space is something many writers, artists, and creative people have. Many need to store the materials they use there. For some it is a haven. For others it is a gift from family that lets them know that they support what they do.

I explored this a long time because I wanted one so badly. I got so many interruptions that I just wanted a place to go and close the door and create things. What I found was these spaces were as individual as a fingerprint. There were kitchens, sitting rooms, art spaces, woodworking shops, his and her shops side by side, converted houses, converted campers, premade cabinets that can open up to create and closed when not in use, sunrooms, backyard retreats, converted garages...the list goes on and on.

The smallest one I found was a closet painted bright pink that barely had room for a chair. The largest ones had multiple zones for a variety of activities. Some were messier than others. Some were made with what was around the house. Others built new from scratch. The array was mind boggling.

I personally had my own sewing room, then a spare bedroom, then a backyard retreat, and a then rented space. Then there was nothing for a long time and I used the kitchen table. Then I had a built in desk nook. Then there was a corner of my bedroom with a glider. When my daughter moved out, she was barely down the street when I started moving stuff into her "old" bedroom. I loved it in there. It felt so spacious for my creative juices to flow. Then my son moved out and I laughed. I had the whole house to myself and didn't really need one anymore.

Right now I still have the creative space for painting and containing my materials but I don't use it that much. As for writing, I am fine with sitting on the couch with my laptop on my lap, a jump drive, and my portable wireless internet I can take anywhere. This is especially handy in hotels that lock their wifi and charge for it. My personal one gets through.

I hope that where ever life leads I can always have a creative space to call my own. Maybe you want that too. What matters is <u>that</u> you create not <u>where</u>.

Know People

A lot of what I learned about writing well centers on people. Over the years in my teaching career I got to do just that. I got to know how people approach so many things. These experiences coupled with writing workshops and feedback is a wonderful thing to make writing real. This has given me insight on perspectives, interests, and ultimately what they might buy.

On Failure

So why would I write a book about writing when I am not formally traditionally published yet? This apparent "failure" has taught me many things that I thought might be useful to someone else. People sometimes appreciate that as they are working on their goal. It is good to have someone else is who is not up there and unreachable. Don't get me wrong, arriving at a destination or reaching a goal is a good thing. Things that come easy don't have the impact that the things we work hard and long on. I see it this way, I haven't really failed because I haven't quit.

I also did not know this dream would keep tapping me on the shoulder again and again. There just has to be something there for me for this to keep happening. I hope that is happening to you too.

Hope

Today I got some hope from an author on the Kindle Direct Publishing site. His name is Barry Eisler a New York Time Best Seller who was unhappy with decisions that were being made about his book that he had no power to change in traditional publishing. He announced that he was considering changing from traditional to self-publishing. Amazon called him. He saw that he could have control over many aspects of his book, partner with Amazon's big muscle ability to mass market and distribute books, get a royalty from 15% to now70% of the cost of each ebook, and get it out quick to his readers. Amazon can handle his millions of readers.

I too saw the possibility and opportunity in all of this a while ago too over that sandwich with that local author. It is good to know Amazon will be right there should I succeed. That opportunity was not there when I started.

Part 5: Uploading Your book to Create Space

Congratulations! You finished a book and want to share it with people. This part of getting it ready for sale is very exciting. This chapter is a "heads up" about what is involved and what you are getting into. I was told by a fellow author that you could do the whole thing for free, and it turned out to be true. Welcome to your new adventure!

Things to do before you log on to Create Space

Write and edit the book. How you have it typed up is how it will appear in your book. The spacing and the font is up to you. I go with the default on the computer. A plain font and 11 or 12 point type is best. Fancy fonts are hard on the reader.

Decide on the size of your book. Choose from the sizes on Create Space. These are all the standard sizes in the book industry. There is an option to make it other sizes too. If you are a forward thinker, consider a standard size because it will fit on the shelf with the other books on the bookshelf in a bookstore. (Yeah, let's think big.) Adjust the size of the page either before or after you have written it. The first time I adjusted the page size after I wrote it, it scared me. I used the "save as" feature on my computer so I could have a copy to play with and the original. It turned out to be just fine. Even on the small pages with margins will adjust to the default size. I never adjust them. This gives enough room for printing and binding your book that Create Space needs.

Add page numbers. Remember that when they print it the page numbers will be right where you put them. They will not automatically adjust in your book. If you put them on the right or the left, they will be on the wrong side every other page. For that reason, I put the page numbers on the center top or bottom.

Add front matter. You make the title page, the copyright page, dedication page and the table of contents. If you change any of the contents you may have to renumber the table of contents. I can't tell you how many times I have had to do that.

Add the index, appendices and author bio in the back. Some people also put their acknowledgements back there. I like that idea. When I buy a book I like to get into to the contents. Putting the acknowledgements in the back gets me into the information faster instead of having to hunt for it.

Go set up the business. You will need a DBA from the county court office, and an EIN. You will need to decide how you are doing business (sole proprietorship, partnership, etc). Amazon needs that info to set up your account. They will also need your routing number and bank account number for your business. They prefer to use automatic deposit to pay your royalties.

Log on to Create Space and set up your Account

You have the choice of making a book, a music recording or a film. Click on the paperback book choice. If you decide to record music or make a film later, those will all appear on your same dashboard.

Click on "start a title for free". Your dashboard will appear. There is a lot of cool information there: Your royalty balance, your projects, and your account information. There is also a community of other self-publishers to help answer questions about using the create space website. There are lots of beginners on there and some good answers. The most reliable one is Create Space's own "contact support". I contact them after I go through their website and can't find out the answer.

Type the title of your project in the space provided. Choose the "guided" set up process. Now the title is on your dashboard. It is a live link that will take you to the project dashboard. The guided set up process has many "What's This?" links that explain things. Even after loading seven books, I still use this set up.

Working with the Dashboard

Each time you log on to Create Space you will go to your project dash board to see what to do next. When you finish a step it gives you the next one or the option to save and move to the next one. It only saves a new page, not each individual item on the page. Each one has to be complete before you can save.

There are 5 major steps to do to release your book. What you will get here is how to do it for free.

Create

I usually skip this stage. You can release the book without doing this step. The options are available later in the set up and on the dashboard, you are not bypassing important information.

Setup

The first step is to give the title information. They need to know the complete title and who the authors are. I have never worked with anyone else so I don't know how they handle more than one author in regards to royalties.

The next step is the ISBN number. You have a choice to make about applying for your own ISBN or being assigned one by Create Space. This is an important decision and can determine the future of your book. There is a fee through the Library of Congress for registering each book. Click around at all the options before deciding to go for the free option. Once you decide, it will be locked.

The interior decisions are made next. You get to decide which color paper and ink. You choose the trim size that I referred to earlier. Then you upload the book file. They prefer a PDF even though there are other options. Click browse and go find your book file. Click on that file. The file will then begin loading. If your connection is not high speed it will not upload. I will indicate when it is complete. Then click "save".

Next, make the cover. Choose your cover paper finish. Then click "Build Your Cover Online". This will take you to "Cover Creator". It has 11 tasks to do. You get to choose a "Theme". Don't be concerned about the color or the photo on it. What you are choosing is the arrangement of text and photos. All the colors and photo choices are yours. The text blocks are in place with jumbled letters. You will want to backspace and type in your information. It will size the text to fit the page. It does not spell check. The cover creator will take your own photos taken with a smart phone that have been uploaded to your computer. The biggest problem I have had with this is making the cover and the interior the same size. It has to be exact. I didn't notice the default size might not be the size of my interior.

The next step is "Complete Setup". This is includes an opportunity to edit and change anything else about your book. There is a statement about the "Review Process" and what they do. It is not much at all. They are looking to see if it will print. That is about it. One of my reviews tried to get me to take the page number 1 off the title page. It just wouldn't. Another said the size of the interior and the cover were not the same size. Please look at it yourself with the online preview feature. It is really cool at how it turns the pages when you click.

Review

The next step is to check it for errors. There are some features there to help you. You can make changes at this time, but I don't. Then I order a proof of my book which costs less if you can wait on the mail, more if you get excited and choose overnight mail.

Distribute

While the proof is coming in the mail, I do this step. Choose your distribution channels, I choose the free ones. Use the calculator to set your price. Amazon is very up front about their cost and then everything else over that is yours. Write your description next. This will appear on Amazon when customers click on your book, just as you type it. Consider uploading it on Kindle. Open a Kindle Direct Publishing account. Then Create Space will convert it to an ebook when you click it on the dashboard. The royalty is higher on Kindle and goes to more countries in the world because it cost them about 2 cents to deliver one of my books.

Sales and Marketing

This is up to you. Even traditional publishing makes you market your own book these days. What Amazon does is make it available to the world and exchanges money into US dollars.

They provide lots of reports to print for your records. They send a 1099 for tax purposes.

One really important piece of information is to learn which tags to use for people to find your book. You get 5. One of my books had a great tag and that helped to sell my book without a lot of marketing. I made friends with a couple of librarians. They are so tech savvy these days. I hope to enlist their help one day as some of my books are hard to describe.

So that is it. It is a process that gets easier over time. They say in business that businesses don't run themselves. I think this one does, to some degree. Much success to you!

Part 6: Ramping it Up to a Creative Life

In 2008 I decided I wanted a creative job. In 2010 I wanted a creative life to go with it. I had no idea how to get from teaching full time to writing full time. I tried so many things and then sadly my summer would end and the little bit of magic I had would fade only to be revived on the next vacation.

A few months ago, I also talked with someone about retirement. She said a lot of people don't give it thought. They retire with no plan, flounder around a while and then they get depressed. She gave me the idea of transitioning myself to something. A creative life is what I chose. It feels so good as I have my studio in a public place now and so many other things going.

I talked with someone else who cautioned me about the creative life that my son has chosen to begin working on. He asked me if I wanted that for him. I gave him an answer but thought about it later, coming up with a better one. Why would I stop him? This is his choice. As someone who chose an alternate plan in teaching I have come to realize that the creative spirit cannot be hidden. And when I did, I came across as a fake and felt like a fake for years on end. It was such an awful feeling that I wanted to run out the door. Why would I want that for him?

My sister in her wisdom as an artist said something the other day about this. She said some people have developed a mature kind of art and they are ready to go into the field of art full time right away. Others need a day job to support themselves for a time as they develop their art. I think I was the second kind. My career in teaching helped me to grow as a person and deal with a variety of situations and develop skills I didn't know I needed then. Being protected by an alternate field just didn't really happen for me. I speculate that coming under fire for being different happened anyway.

Fuel to Go Big and On My Own

It all seemed to come together most recently when the pressure was on to do and be who I am not. That gave me fuel for this new venture I didn't have before. I sat down at my computer and expanded my writing to include an educational component. Yes, I would teach people what I know after working with this for nearly 35 years. Certainly it could give people a start. I decided it would be realistic. It would involve enjoying writing and putting it out there. It would be fun. I would not make promises to them I could not keep.

I checked out all the avenues I had located and checked into before about making a writing business go. Interestingly, all of them were open. I rented a small office space in a building I had looked at before. I wanted my writing venture to feel like going to work. I wanted to take it seriously and to have something to do when I am not working. As I went, it took on an urgency that is hard to describe. In two weeks I had it fully furnished and ready to work there.

SCORE Workshop

I then took the beginning small business seminar from SCORE, an organization of retired business men and women. I found out about them from the Small Business Administration several years ago. I drove over to one of their centers awhile back to ask some questions and they suggested the seminar. I went hoping that I knew a little more than I thought and they might plug in the holes for me about what I didn't. It turned out to be true. What I got was a whole list of things to do and a new word: micro entrepreneur. This type of business outsources some of the work to someone else like I do with Amazon. They really do save me lots of time and money to publish on demand through Create Space and Kindle Direct Publishing. They take out a lot of the risk and give me access to the world.

I am charging through my list and putting this business in place. It is very long. It is also what business people do. Already it is taking the guesswork out of it and preventing myself from those wandering detours I so often take on my creative journeys. It feels good.

Gathering My Tribe

I am meeting with a colleague from work that does this too. We have been talking about this in little conversations as we bump into each other. She gave me some cool resources and I didn't have a pencil to write them down so I invited her for tea at a local coffee shop. She said yes. We swapped stories of what we do and resources. She had given me resources so freely before I came with some to give her. It was a fun get together.

There are a few other people that I need to make this go. A venture like this needs advisory members who are not family, as they said at the SCORE workshop, people who could offer me business guidance. I think too I need creative people who make a living doing what they love and people who do their art anyway with hope for getting to make a living creatively.

Slowly the people are coming and going in and out of my life. At this point, even a small amount of contact with a creative person is like gold to me.

Uncertainty

This venture can get scary as I think about going it alone and doing what I love to do. I keep at it and doing something every day. Some days I do more. The thing I cannot do is let it freeze me and stop. The more I put myself out there, the more opportunity I give it, the more the life I desire gets a chance to happen. I know others are doing it. I know I can too. My writing studio is full of all the things I love that remind me of that.

Developing Online Classes

I am taking what I know about writing and self-publishing and making online classes of my own. I learned how to do this on my day job. This is different as I get to teach what I want to for the first time in many years. I get to choose the content and what I have them do. I get to answer the questions I had as a beginning self-publisher. It is so cool to have found the Coursecraft website. It is especially for lifelong learners.

As my colleague put it, you only have to teach it once. The relief in this alone had really interested me. There is a particular class that I have taught traditionally 45 times. Class sizes were from 10-30 people each time. That is a ridiculous amount of teaching and very inefficient. The maximum number of students in this online course website is 100 and can be upgraded to include more. I have a plan to offer an "open workshop" at my writing studio so if there are local and still don't get it, we can meet and I will help them in person one on one or in small groups.

Because of the internet, it has helped with the question of traveling to promote this new work I do. I have decided not to. I live in a place with a mild climate and easy to access. People can come and see the sights too if they decide to come and work with me on something.

On the Horizon

My dream of a creative life with a creative job is on the horizon.
I can see it and feel it coming. It is just what I need to do. It is a
lot of work but doesn't feel like work. It is a pleasure to come to
my writing studio as often as I can. I had an Open House
recently at my studio. Two people came. Two other people
wished they could. It was such a lovely time to be supported for
my dream that is out of my head and in real life. Everyone that
has seen it so far likes it. It is the best match for me because I
designed it myself, just for me. One day real soon I am going to
walk away from my old life into this new creative one. Until
then, I am going to work as hard as I can.

For You the Aspiring Writer

I wish you much success in this dream of yours. Leave no stone unturned. Learn much. Take it at the pace that is right for you. There is something wonderful about expressing yourself that someone needs or you would not have the desire to spend so much time writing it. It was put there for a reason. Best of luck. Hope to see you out on the trail!

Susan Napoli

Resources

<u>Introduction</u>

I have included resources that might help in your quest to write a book that I found helpful. I have been doing this a long time so these are my current favorites and those that stood the test of time. Many I don't really have anymore, especially the ones on writing for children. That dream was brought to life again recently when Amazon released a new program for making children's ebooks in picture book format. Don't forget to enjoy yourself as this progresses for you.

Appendix A: Annotated Bibliography

Essential Reference Books

Writer's Market by Writer's Digest Books. Get the current year. If it is a few months before the new edition comes out, don't get it. All the information will be too old. It has some of every genre in there. A good resource to find a publisher. Anything by Writer's Digest Books is good, helpful, and packed with information. They have magazines too that focus on just a few aspects of writing at a time.

Ross, M. and Collier, S. The Complete Guide to Self-Publishing. I used this book to guide me in my first self-publishing venture. It has everything you need form start to finish. The directions are great. Very detailed account of the Business side of Self-Publishing and exactly what you need to do.

Canfield, J. The Success Principles: How to Get From Where You are to Where You Want to Be. A Step by step method on how to get real success by learning what it takes to succeed. Very Challenging and helpful.

Creative Process and Creative Life

Bayles, D. and Orland, T. Art and Fear: observations of the Perils (and rewards) of Artmaking. This book can help pinpoint the reason for not creating or releasing the things you make for people to see.

Cameron, J. The Artist's Way: a Spiritual Path to Higher Creativity. Her first book on creativity that helps to unstuck creative people or uncover their creative side. There are two more that go with this one. All three titles are bound together in one large volume. She has other books too that are worth the read.

Dillard, A. <u>Give It All, Give It Now: One of the Few Things I Know About Writing</u>. A short, beautiful book about not saving anything for another book or holding back for any reason. Encouraging.

Freeman-Zachery, R<u>. Living the creative Life: Ideas and Inspiration from Working Artists</u>. The reader gets a glimpse of the variety of projects and work an artist does to make a living by having multiple things going. The idea of having a creative "tribe" for support is in it too.

Hall, D<u>. Lifework</u>. A journal like view of an author's creative life in the day to day things he does to make a living as a freelance writer.

Keith, K. <u>Do it Anyway</u>. This is a follow your heart's desire book that is an encouraging read on the path to personal meaning.

Kieves, T. <u>This Time I Dance!: Creating the Work You Love</u>. This is an account of a woman who quit her job as a lawyer to become a writer. It has the steps she took and the struggles she faced. Funny. Encouraging.

McMeekin, G. <u>The 12 Secrets of Highly Creative Women: a portable mentor</u>. Interviews with women about their creative lives. Has a chart of interests of creative women. Lots of great quotes in the margins on creativity.

Phillips, J. <u>Marry Your Muse: Making a Lasting Commitment to Your Creativity</u>. This is a complete course in creative expression. I love the spiritual aspect of creativity in this book and her insights on being original.

For the Rich and Famous Track

Ban Breathbach, Sarah. <u>Peace and Plenty: finding your path to financial Serenity</u>. This book is a shocking account of how a New York Times Best seller lost every dime of the money she made and all the lessons she learned. Heart breaking. It is like sitting down to tea with her and hearing what it is really like to be a rich and famous author.

Stanley, T.J. and Danko, W.D. <u>The Millionaire Next Door: the surprising account of America's wealthy</u>. A study of how millionaires really live and what they buy. A must read.

<u>Who Does She Think She Is?</u> Video and kit. (aired on PBS).

Writing Humor about not making it

MacLeod, H. <u>Ignore Everybody and 39 Other Keys to Creativity</u>. This is advice from a working author that takes a don't sweat it approach and do what you please approach to writing. He also turned a blog into this book and told how it all happened.

Pierre, S. <u>The Artist in the Office: How to Creatively Survive and Thrive Seven Days a Week</u>. This book is in a cartoon format and what it is like to be creative in a corporate workplace with creative work on the side and rather not have it that way.

Walsh, P. <u>78 Reasons Why Your Book May Never Be Published and 14 Reasons Why it Just Might</u>. A dose of reality approach to writing. A compelling read that I could not put down.

Business Magazines

Success.

Entrepreneur.

Business Books

Entrepreneur Press. <u>How to Start a Business in Texas</u>

Mladjenovic, P. <u>Micro-Entrepreneurship for Dummies</u>

Creative Workspaces

All these books are an explosion of pictures of creative spaces of all kinds with the exception of M. Maisel's book. Each book is visual delight, every one of them. Where Women Create is also a magazine that comes out four times a year as does Studios.

Better Homes and Gardens. <u>Studio Spaces</u>.

Freeman-Zachery, R. <u>Creative Time and Space</u>.

Madden, C. <u>A Room of Her Own</u>.

Maisel, E. A Writer's Space: <u>Make Room to Dream, to Work, To Write.</u>

Packham, Jo. <u>Where Women Create</u>.

Perrella. L. <u>Art Making and Studio Spaces</u>.

Cloth, Paper, Scissors. Studios (magazine).

Appendix B: Magazine Articles on Writing

"JK Rowling Reads for the Magic". O The Oprah Magazine. January 2001. An interview after her first book.

"How to Get Unstuck" by Lisa Dierbeck. O The Oprah Magazine. January 2005. How she unblocked a major writer's block.

"Are Your Goals Holding You Back?" O the Oprah Magazine. November 2005. The key to happiness lies in checking out the detours and back roads.

"How to Plot a Children's Story" by Jane McBride Choate. The Writer. December 2005.

"Inside the Writer's Mind" O the Oprah magazine. August 2007. 6 novelists tells you what it takes.

"This Year You Write Your Novel" by Walter Mosley. O The Oprah Magazine. August 2007.

"Escape Your Rat Race"by Martha Beck. O the Oprah Magazine, January 2009. Good advice for when you don't know what to do next.

"Chance of a Lifetime" O The Oprah Magazine. February 2009. A look at luck.

"Some Thoughts on Writing" by Elizabeth Gilbert. From her website: Elizabethgilbert.com

"Who Needs a Publisher?" by Isa Jasiewicz. Newsweek. 2010. In the DIY era, putting out your own book is no longer an act of vanity.

"Wabi Sabi Your Life". 2010. Whole Living Magazine a Martha Stewart Publication. Simple Strategies for embracing imperfection.

"Make Your Own Luck" by Rebecca Webber. Psychology Today. May/June 2010. Five principles for making the most of life's twists, turns and coincidences.

"One Wild and Precious Life" O The Oprah Magazine April 2012. Maria Shriver visits the famously private Mary Oliver, poet.

Appendix C: Free Marketing, Learning and Self-Publishing Sources

Facebook: a free social network that allows you to have a business page in addition to a personal page.

Twitter: a free social network to give readers short up to the minute goings on of you and your book.

You Tube: a free venue to upload videos to promote your book. They do monetize after you get enough views.

Blogger: a free Google blog venue that you can write blogs that could become books. Can monetize your blog if you get advertizing.

Good Reads: An Amazon company that allows you to set up an author page and get free reviews.

Createspace: an Amazon company that prints on demand books, videos or music for indie creators. Up front business practices, monthly reports online, free distribution. Let's you create and they do the leg work.

Kindle Direct Publishing: an Amazon ebook company that is on demand and available worldwide.

Kindle Kids Book Creator: an Amazon product for producing ebooks in a picture book format for children.

Leisure Learning Unlimited: an opportunity to teach and get paid for what you know that is linked to your book.

Zazzle: an on demand merchandise company that readers can order products that promote your books (t-shirts, coffee cups, etc).

SCORE: a free resource of business advice from retired businessmen and women associated with the Small Business Administration. They have centers to learn more about any aspect of running a business including marketing. There is a library of reading materials. There are free one on one consultation sessions. All services are free except some of the workshops have a small fee and they serve food. They are extremely helpful and knowledgeable. They want to see you succeed.

Guilds: Check out the writer's guild or the associated genre guild. They are not free but provide good information at their conferences. At this writing, there is one locally for $190 for non-members for three days. In my estimation, that is extremely reasonable for what you get there as I have attended a few before. There are publishing companies represented there, workshop sessions, a chance to rub elbows with all kinds of people who write and sell books. There is a bit of a divide between the published and the unpublished there but don't let that bother you. Loaded with information.

Kickstarter: A website where people give you money to finance your dream. Must be well planned. If it doesn't work out, the donations go back to the donors. If it does, then you got a success on your hands.

Acknowledgements

Thank you Denise Shead author of <u>Golden Christmas</u> and her daughter Holly Bankston for letting me tag along the book signing night at the coffee shop and our conversations. You inspired me to write this book.

Thank you to Keith Stein of the SCORE team who offered information and enthusiasm about starting a business.

Thank you to Beth Hammett for your openness to share ideas about writing.

Thank you to Carla Anderson for your enthusiasm, laughter and fun conversations.

Thank you Mayuko Ono Grey and Mark Greenwalt both artists and super creative people. Thanks for the conversations about art, creativity and glimpses into the art world.

About the Author

Susan Devine Napoli has been an indie author since 1980. She is a mother of two adult children and a new grandmother of 1 grandchild. She lives with three cats in Houston, TX.

You can write to or tour her public writing studio: 1120 Nasa Parkway Suite 220U, Houston, TX 77058.

Announcements and activities are posted to her public Facebook page SN Books. Her current books can be found on her author page on Amazon.com. You can contact her via email napolisnpw@aol.com. It goes to her phone and is checked throughout the day, most days.

She does not accept engagements that involve traveling at this time.